CALIFORNIA WOMEN VOTE!!

A Fight That Never Should Have Been Necessary

by

gay toltl kinman

Editor: Patricia Allen Smith
Cover: Peggie Chan
Photo of gay toltl kinman: Brian and Lilly Loo Studios
Interfacing with Kindle and Amazon: Peggie Chan

Published in the United States of America
By Mysterious Women

Well-behaved women seldom make history.

~Louise Thatcher Ulrich

Nothing is impossible to organized womanhood –united in aim and effort.

~Caroline Seymour Severance

Also by gay toltl kinman

MYSTERY NOVELS

Smotherings: An LAPD Officer Agnes Graham Mystery Novella
The Lido Libretto
The Shooter Mystery Short Stories Series
Greenway - Four Mystery Short Stories Set on Greenway, Agatha Christie's Holiday Home in Devon
Death in San Antonio Mystery Stories: Four mystery short stories set in San Antonio featuring P.I. Brooke
Jo Peters Mysteries: Cases as Assistant District Attorney, City Attorney & P.I.
Tony Reynolds, CIA Agent: Cozy Thriller Stories
Vengeance Is Mine: Nine cases that are based on real cases—but with a twist
A Man Of Honor: A Marlowe and LAPD Officer Agnes Graham Mystery
Stand Down, Mystery Stories
Death in Hollywood 1942: The Marlowe & LAPD Officer Agnes Graham Series
Death in...17 Mysteries
Death in Hamburg
Murder and Mayhem at The Huntington Library
Wolf Castle (originally published as Castle Reiner)
Death in Rancho Las Amigas
Upclose and Personal
Death in Covent Garden
Death in A Small Town

CHILDREN'S MYSTERIES

The Adventures of Lauren Macphearson
Lauren Macphearson and The Scottish Adventure
Lauren Macphearson and The Colorado Adventure
Lauren Macphearson and The Jumbled Cupboard Adventure
Lauren Macphearson and The Ghostly Adventure

Super Sleuth: Five Alison Leigh Powers Mysteries
The Mystery of The Missing Arabian
The Mystery of The Missing Miniature Books
The Mystery of The Octagon House
The Secret of The Equestrian Park
The Secret of The Strange Staircase

Divorce or Don't Make The Mistakes I Did
The Mystery at The Stables
The Mystery at The Rodeo Ranch

NON-FICTION

Desserticide II: AKA Just Desserts and Deathly Advice
Gilly's Manual and Advice on Coping with Your Divorce
Hidden Heroines of The Huntington

PLAYS

The Play's The Thing: A Collection of Plays
A Little Theater Mystery
Death In Russia
Putting Mother's Seat Belt On
Revenge
The Audition
The Mystery Writer
The Thief
Wicked Well
The Purloined Letter
Not One More Word
The Ashes of Zane Grey
Baskets to Jade
Esther Howland: Queen Of Hearts
(A Ten-Minute Biographical Play)
Esther Howland: Queen Of Hearts
(A One-Act Biographical Play)
Nicholas Owen: Builder Of Secret Places
(A Ten-Minute Biographical Play)
Nicholas Owen: Finder Of Secret Places
(A One-Act Biographical Play)
Home Sweet Murder
Mr. Marshall's Doppelganger
The Deposition
Unscheduled Changeover in Hamburg 1974

AUDIOBOOKS

Death in a Small Town
Death in Rancho Las Amigas
Up Close and Personal

ACKNOWLEDGEMENTS

It takes a village to produce a book. My deepest gratitude is to The Huntington Library for its unique collection of California suffrage material, and for the care and enthusiasm in which the staff served, not only me, but all the other Readers and Scholars. My many thanks to:

David Mihaley

Jennifer A. Watts

Hector Acosta

Barbara Alvarado Gyorgyovich

Morex Arai

Stephanie Arias

Adrian Aviles

Lisa Caprino

Ariana Celis

Nate De Gala

Mark Fleming

Lo Hom

Leslie Jobsky

James Kitahara

Mide Kolawole

Wendy Maciel

Mina Marciano

Rosa Mazon

Kevin Miller

Emily Neis

Madeline Northcote-Smith

Frank Osen

Jazmin Rew-Pinchem

Edward Rivas

Karina Sanchez

Mariella Seltzer

Addy Stupin

Erica Wofford

A big thanks to fellow critiquers Meredith Taylor and Susan Rowland,

and to editor Patricia Allen Smith,

and to interfacer and cover artist Peggie Chan,

and to the writing organizations I belong to: Society of Children's Book Writers and Illustrators, Mystery Writers of America, Sisters in Crime, Historical Novel Society, Short Mystery Fiction Society, and the Private Eye Writers of America—another community of caring and helpful members.

TABLE OF CONTENTS

CHAPTER ONE
THE ANTIS
ARGUMENTS AGAINST WOMEN VOTING

[California 1911. Opposition to Ballot Measure #8 amending the California Constitution to allow women to vote was distributed on leaflets in advance of the election on October 10, 1911. The only people allowed to vote at the time were white males over the age of 21. There were 23 constitutional amendments on the ballot.]

VOTERS! Do NOT Vote for the Woman Suffrage Amendment!

Whereas: We, the women of California, Mothers, Wives and Sisters, home-lovers and home-makers, believe that we can best serve our country, our State and society, at large, by living our lives according to the laws of our being, as the Creator made us, within the sphere where He has placed us, and not in seeking to thrust ourselves into a sphere foreign to woman's nature and inclination and beyond her capabilities, such as the public area, for which man is physically and intellectually better adapted, fitted, and suited than women; and we believe that the best way to purify politics is to make our husbands, sons and brothers good citizens by giving them the influence of a home-center where love and domestic harmony prevail, and to which end a woman's efforts and endeavors must needs be constant and unflagging;

We believe that the mixing and meddling in politics and the consequent publicity and notoriety must and will of necessity, rob a woman of her most precious dower, and natural endowments: viz: those of dignity, modesty and womanly reserve, and tend to coarsen and cheapen her;

We, the women of California, stand as heretofore, active, willing and ready to perform all duties to our community and in every department of civic life compatible with womanliness, whenever and wherever woman's influence and co-operation are called for and required;

We, the women of California, as above-named, respectfully plead with the honorable body of voters in the State of California, that they do not thrust upon us the most unwelcome burden of the ballot and all it must involve, we, feeling ourselves unfit to bear it or to perform the incidental duties, in addition to those most engrossing which we are already pledged to fulfil in all conscientiousness and honor, in our present capacity of wives, mothers and sisters of the State of California.

And in consequence of our belief and convictions we most earnestly ask, and urge, that the honorable body of

VOTERS, Do NOT Vote for the Woman Suffrage Amendment!

Other arguments on the Antis' side:

- It would destroy the home.
- Unwomanly.
- Mothers would neglect their children.
- Wives would divorce their husbands over political disagreements.
- It would be a vote for organized female nagging forever.
- To engage in politics would taint and soil a woman's purity and goodness and unsex her.
- Women are inferior to men in physical and mental development.
- Women are more emotional than men.
- For a woman to run a household, bear and rear children requires little or no education.
- Every married woman would receive protection and support from her husband.
- If women got the right to vote, they would shut down the liquor industry.
- Women don't want the ballot.
- Women's votes would change the family and alter the relationship of the sexes, making women mannish and undermining the status and masculinity of man.

- Women are content with their lives so they don't want to vote.
- Women would not use the vote if they had it.
- Women would neglect their homes, desert their families and spend all their time at the polls.
- If they had the vote, they would vote the same as their husbands. Which would only double the existing vote. If they voted against their husbands, they would create discord, family quarrels and divorce.
- Women are angels. Or women are depraved and would introduce into politics a vicious element that would ruin our national life.
- Women cannot understand politics so if they had the vote, they wouldn't know what to do with it.
- Women cannot band together. They are incapable of organization so if they had the vote they would band together on one side and the men on the other. A sex war would follow that might end in bloody revolution.
- The ballot is overrated. It has never done anything for anybody. The ballot is what makes man a man. What gives him all his dignity and his superiority to women. If women shared this privilege, how could a woman look at her own husband? There would be nothing to look at.
- Women are represented already by their husbands, fathers and brothers.
- Women are represented by the men in their families, so they don't need to vote.
- If the laws are unjust, they can be corrected by women's indirect influence.
- The bad women would outvote the good ones.
- Women don't understand politics. Or business. Businessmen do and are better fitted to run a city or a state.
- Women would lose their influence—which they have through beauty, goodness, tact, talent, pleasant manners, money, social position, etc.
- Too many voters. There are already too many voters.

- Would unsex woman. It will turn women into men.
- The women's club movement began in 1868 with weekly meetings to discuss questions of interest to women. Many believe that discussing politics, specifically the voting issue, was detrimental to a woman's modesty and the interest of the home.
- Suffragists were looked upon as dangerous radicals and condemned as unladylike.
- Let well enough alone.
- Having the vote would corrupt a woman's morals, weaken her nature and destroy her finer instincts. Leave the voting for the boys.
- Some fathers were disturbed because they feared men would teach women too much old machine politics.
- One Congressman stated that he would give the vote to spinsters and widows but not married women. *Can not a wife trust her husband to represent her. If not, why? Is the husband not mentally qualified to do so? Get a divorce, get a sane man and marry. I will vote to exclude the married women.*
- An article in The Utopian stated: *Whenever a woman enters the political area, she sacrifices the charm of womanhood, delicacy of manner, which cannot be kept pure under the coarse contaminating influence....We do not assert that politics is degrading to women, but we do think it does not elevate, neither do we think women wield the purifying influence at the polls as suffrage advocates claim...the better class of women care little for the ballot or political honors, feeling that 'the hand that rocks the cradle rules the world,' that the mother who gives to her state is sufficient....The true woman who would make the most of her every God-given attribute asks not for the ballot, but for love, and home, where the carols of babyhood are sung to the sweetest of babies, where home is heaven and where the weary husband may find rest and aching hearts sympathy.*
- Mormon scholar B. H. Roberts stated that suffrage should be granted only to those who could act independently and without dictation. No woman under twenty-one years of age should be allowed to vote. Married women could not act independently. *By all the laws of nature, spoken through the words of God, man is the head of*

the woman. I do not believe that this headship means tyranny and oppression. Woman was not taken from the head of man for fear she might rule over him, but from under his arm that he might protect her, such is the natural rule.... The franchise has always been given as a matter of protection. Do our wives, mothers, sisters and daughters need protection against us?

- Tavern associations and brewers and distillers were against suffrage because of the close ties between votes for women and votes for Prohibition. Politicians feared shifting district demographics. Scientists—even some of the best—argued that women didn't have the mental capacity needed to make informed voting decisions. Husbands and fathers either felt that the votes of their wives and daughters would be redundant—or feared that they wouldn't. Women want to keep to their sphere—the home and family where their influence was felt every day.
- Anti-suffrage actions were shown in mocking political cartoons and posters, harangues from the pulpit, and propaganda in the forms of articles and op-eds that professed the views of the anti-suffrage faction.
- Fear mongering and ridicule were frequent parts of the fight to defeat woman suffrage.
- The Catholic Church, which had a heavy influence on the formerly Spanish territory, openly opposed woman suffrage in the nineteenth century, and the culture of male machismo in the region further stymied any attempts for discussions of women's rights.
- Chinese men [who had the vote] disliked the idea of self-governing women and were easily convinced the measure would give women so much freedom that the Chinese culture would be threatened.
- The *Los Angeles Times* in an article dated January 21, 1911, stated: *Women are incapable of physically dominating men. By their inferior physical strength, they are unable to compete on an equal basis in any line of endeavor where ability is determined by sheer bodily prowess. All positions of physical power—such as in our police forces, our armies and our navies—will necessarily be filled by men. In other words, the enforcement of all law must inevitably rest with men. No law or ordinance could be effectually upheld except through*

the willingness of men to uphold it. And no matter what words were written on the statute books of any state, if the physical power (which is the masculine power) behind it were withdrawn, the law would immediately become void and impotent. Therefore, in equal suffrage we have the spectacle of women trying to pass laws which they are physically incapable of upholding, and laws which they admit the men do not want.

Then on June 19, 1911, the *Times* continued:

Possession of the ballot will not help women, socially or industrially. It will make exactions upon her time and strength. It will invade the home and destroy its charm. It will not result in wiser laws or better government.

- The *Times* stated that it opposes woman suffrage because it does not believe in either the justice or the expediency of burdening the women of California with the duty of voting.

  On October 1, 1911, Democratic State Senator J.B. Sanford in a Times opinion piece called woman's suffrage a disease, a political hysteria, a cruel and intolerable burden, and a backward step in the progress of civilization. And he further stated: It is the mannish female politician and the little effeminate, sissy man, and the woman who is dissatisfied with her lot and sorry that she was born a woman.

- At a state political convention of 1901, Mrs. Benjamin Fay Mills, a Christian socialist whose husband was a noted speaker for Christian socialism, *asserted that the new woman should have the obligation of the ballot....I hope that they will not get into politics, as it is not what they should be in until there is something in it more worthy of right-thinking, progressive people.*

- Many cartoons portrayed women in bloomers as beer-drinking cigar-smokers employed in so-called 'male' jobs, like driving a cab. Meanwhile, their husbands were shown in dresses, tending to their children.

- *Prediction that women would refuse to vote, or they would vote as their men folk doubling representation or vote against them and disrupt the family. They would put up unfit women for office and support them, they would be prey of politicians and...would not take the trouble to comprehend complex issues or they would demand foolish moral measures evolved from their own emotional nature.*

- Senator J.B. Sanford stated: *Mr. Voter: How would you like to come home some evening and find the children dirty and hungry; no supper for you and "Wifey" locked up in a jury-room with eleven men? This is what women suffrage means. Vote no October 10 on Senate Amendment No. 8—the Equal Suffrage Amendment, the fourth one on the ballot.*
- The Washington State Territorial Dispatch insisted that *it is a mistake to call Miss Anthony a Reformer or the movement in which she is engaged as a reform; she is a Revolutionist, aiming at nothing less than the breaking up of the very foundations of society and overthrow of every social institution....the whole plan is coarse, sensual and agrarian, the worst phase of French infidelity and communism.*
- Many men did not want any change in the way the government at all levels was functioning. Who knew what effect would result from having so many more people vote?
- Politicians asked how women would vote. If they divided along the same lines as men, then candidates and legislation in the major parties saw no benefit to change the law. To the extent women might support new parties favoring moral reform, then they were a potential threat.
- From a pamphlet published by the Woman's Anti-Suffrage Association of Massachusetts. *Housewives: You do not need the vote to wash out your sink spout. A handful of potash and some boiling water is quicker and cheaper.*
- *Your wife is elected to Legislature and your daughter is elected constable and you are at home taking care of the babies.* Statement by James Caples, Sacramento delegate, Second Constitutional Convention, 1879.

CHAPTER TWO
FACTS

FACT: Taxation without representation is tyranny.

FACT: The concept of the Constitution and Bill of Rights date from 1776. The United States was formed because its inhabitants were paying taxes but could not vote for their representatives—who happened to be Englishmen in England.

FACT: When the United States was formed the men could vote. What all citizens had dearly fought for—the vote—was denied to women, almost half of the population, many of whom paid taxes.

FACT: The laws were made by men for men.

FACT: In the United States whatever a woman had when she came to the marriage became the man's. Widows had more privileges. Women could not sign contracts or own property.

FACT: In California women could own property and pay taxes but they could not vote. Owning property was part of the Hispanic heritage in the laws of California.

FACT: Fathers were sole guardians under California law. Joint guardianship bills failed in 1909 and 1911. Only unmarried women could hold property, engage in business and will property when deceased—just the same as a man.

FACT: A married woman took the citizenship of her husband, not the other way around. However, a woman could apply for citizenship without the consent of her husband.

FACT: A wife could hold separate property, which she could control up to a point. The community property was under the control of the husband. He could only will half of it; however she could not will away any of it. She only had use of it during her lifetime. The husband could sell the property without the wife's signature, but she couldn't sell it without his signature. Her separate property was liable for his debts.

FACT: In 1891, Clara Shortridge Foltz, the first woman lawyer in California, and Laura DeForce Gordon, also a lawyer, were able to get a bill passed giving women the right to vote in school elections. It was vetoed by the Governor.

FACT: The community property law was changed so that a husband could not dispose of community property without his wife's consent. This was nullified by the California Supreme Court.

FACT: In 1904 Black men could vote but women of all races could not.

FACT: In the fight for the vote interruptions came, such as the Civil War and the World War I.

FACT: From 1896-1910 the United States Supreme Court took the phrase *all men are created equal* literally. It ruled that the protection under the United States Constitution did not include women.

FACT: Ellen R. Van Valkenburg, 43 and a widow, sued the California Santa Cruz County Clerk Albert Brown after he refused to include her name in the county's Great Register of Voters. She argued that under the Fourteenth Amendment to the United States Constitution, women were granted citizenship and therefore the rights of voting were included. California's Third District Appeals Court ruled against her. As did the California Supreme Court denying her and all women the right to vote.

FACT: An 1895 United States Supreme Court ruling stated that voting was not a right of citizenship.

FACT: *We, the people* includes the female of the species.

FACT: Other countries in the world had voting rights for women. In Iceland in 1911 women over 25 could vote. In 1915 all women could vote there.

FACT: Virginia Minor tried to vote in Missouri. She was arrested, appealed and her case went to the United States Supreme Court. Her argument was that the right to vote was part of the rights of a citizen. The Court said the Constitution did not allow women to vote—which meant that women needed an amendment to the Constitution. A senator from California in 1874 introduced one in the United States Senate written by Susan B. Anthony which read: *Citizens of the United States to vote shall not be denied...by the United States or any state on account of sex.*

FACT: A woman did vote on November 3, 1868 in California. Charley Darkey Parkhurst 1812-1879 lived her life as a man.

FACT: Women did not have the right to sue their husbands for battery or physical abuse,

FACT: Women could not acquire separate state citizenship rights, which were further abridged in 1907 by the Expatriation Act, which said that if a woman married a foreigner, she forfeited her United State citizenship and took the citizenship of her husband automatically.

FACT: By 1881 school voting rights had been enacted in seven more states. In getting out the women's vote in school elections, the suffragists were able to counter the cry of the antis that *women don't want to vote.*

FACT: In 1870 African American men had the right to vote in the Fourteenth Amendment to the United States Constitution. Those against expanding the vote feared that white male political control would be threatened and did much to stop black men from voting.

FACT: Being a citizen did not entitle one to vote. Is it a right or a privilege or a responsibility? The United States Supreme Court had ruled on the citizen issue. At stakes was the definition of the word 'citizen' deemed not to encompass all rights—specifically that of voting.

FACT: Ellen Sergeant brought a suit asking for a refund on her tax as she could not vote. Taxation without representation was unconstitutional, she argued.

FACT: One suffrage poster quotes Abraham Lincoln. *I go for all sharing the privileges of the government who assist in the bearing its burden, by no means excluding women.* [Actually, the original quote is: *I go for all sharing the privileges of the government who assist in bearing its burdens. Consequently, I go for admitting all whites to the right of suffrage who pay taxes or bear arms, by no means excluding females.*]

FACT: Susan B. Anthony was fined for registering to vote—a federal offense. She refused to pay the fine and was jailed. But not for long—as her fine was paid by a supporter. She was upset by that because she wanted to go to jail to publicize the injustice of the voting system.

FACT: In campaigning against suffrage, some women broke their own rule of moving out of their home sphere to actively work against women getting the right to vote.

FACT: The California Secretary of State Blue Book of 1908 reads: *Persons excluded from the Suffrage are Chinese, idiots, insane, persons convicted of embezzlement or infamous crime.* Women were in the same category.

FACT: A woman in California owned a fruit ranch. All of her workers could vote on laws that could affect her business—but she couldn't.

FACT: Up to the early years of the 1900s, a man could give away his wife's children, even children yet unborn. No married woman had a right to the money she earned. No woman could collect for damages to her person or reputation. Few were admitted to institutions of higher learning. No woman could vote, serve on a jury or hold office.

FACT: Mary Wollstonecraft stated: *Women are not creatures with a defect of sex.*

FACT: The penalty for stealing a girl was five years in prison—the same for stealing a pig. However, ten years in prison was the punishment for stealing a mule or a calf.

FACT: The states in which women were able to vote were: Wyoming 1869; Colorado 1893; Utah and Idaho 1896; and Washington State 1910. California would be the sixth star in the suffragist flag. Kansas, Arizona and Oregon followed in 1912, with the Alaska Territory soon thereafter.

FACT: Emperor Justinian (529-560 CE) in his laws (Code of Justinian) stated that freeborn women were citizens, but could not vote or hold political office.

FACT: By 1918 women could vote for the president in 21 states.

FACT: Elizabeth Cady Stanton, 80, wrote *The Woman's Bible,* citing all the sections that degrade women. The first volume was published in 1895 and the second in 1898. Both parts give the female view of the religious orthodoxy that woman should be subservient to man. She contends that a book that makes woman the author of sin, curses her maternity, degrades her in marriage and makes her a mere afterthought in creation cannot have emanated from the great good Spirit of the universes but from the brain of fallible man.

Stanton wanted a critical study of biblical texts that are used to degrade and to subject women as lower beings than men. The volumes are an expose of how traditional patriarchal Christianity and Judaism used scripture to oppress women—and minorities—by deliberate mistranslations, omissions, and twisting the words for men's own gains.

She states: *The Bible teaches woman brought death and sin into the world, that she precipitated the fall of the races, that she was arraigned before the judgement seat of Heaven, tried, condemned and sentenced.*

FACT: The clergy was a major force that controlled women's moral energies and kept pietistic activism from becoming political activism.

FACT: Women had no legal rights to challenge beatings by drunken husbands. For this reason, the temperance movement was in many ways a movement for women's rights.

FACT: Suffrage comes from the Latin *suffragium*, which means *vote, political support or the right to vote.* It was used in the United States Constitution written in 1787 in Article V: *no state without its consent shall be deprived of its equal suffrage in the Senate.* This means that no state will be deprived of its equal rights to vote in the Senate.

The word 'suffrage' has no relation to the word 'suffer.' Although it was certainly an appropriate term as women did suffer.

FACT: The word *franchise* comes from the French language which means *freedom, right, or privilege.* To exercise the franchise means to vote.

FACT: Wyoming, Utah, Colorado and Idaho were the first to allow women the right to vote. Men outnumbered women significantly in these sparsely inhabited territories. Many believed that extending suffrage to women would attract them to the region, start families and build permanent communities.

FACT: No college would admit women until Ohio's Oberlin College had a special program in 1833; California in 1870. No schools of medicine or law admitted women. Stanford University opened as co-educational but limited the number of women who could attend. No limit on the number of men. Yale did not accept women until 1968.

CHAPTER THREE
WOMEN'S CLUBS

Let's time travel and fly like an eagle over the entire United States to quickly view the highlights of the women's club history

Nothing happens in a vacuum. That doesn't mean the carpet cleaning one. It means nothing happens without preceding events.

In the 1830s—about 60 years after the Declaration of Independence—women began to get together informally—although it was frowned upon to do so. Women had their place—the so-called 'sphere,' namely the home, that many claimed was stated in the Bible. Their time was not to be taken away from their place in their 'sphere' just to be with other women.

Early women's organization had been religious in purpose, meeting in churches, learning more about the Bible and moral improvement. Social mores would not allow any other kind of groups. Church groups were one of the few socially-sanctioned ways women were initially allowed to meet outside of the home.

Quilting bees grew out of church groups where women could get together, be industrious and produce something that was useful. This was considered an acceptable extension of woman's 'sphere' by the menfolk and the church officials.

Women needed the companionship of other women, as we do today.

Women wanted to learn. But institutions of higher learning did not admit women, nor were they encouraged to leave their 'sphere.' Boys and men were the ones who earned degrees so they could better provide for their families—when they had them. The women were needed at home, where large families were the norm. Besides, why did a woman need an education to cook, clean and take care of children? That was the prevalent thinking of the time.

The first major recorded push for women's rights in the United States came in 1848, before the Civil War, in Seneca Falls, when Elizabeth

Cady Stanton presented the *Woman's Bill of Rights.* Suffrage for women was on the list of goals.

Stanton, in particular, felt that religious organizations held women back and discriminated against them. Many years later she wrote *The Woman's Bible* highlighting the passages that demean women. She gathered together a group of women scholars to view the original texts.

For example, Part 1 is the *Pentateuch* with comments on *Genesis, Exodus, Leviticus Numbers and Deuteronomy.* She states in the Preface:

The object is to revise only those texts and chapters referring to women, and those also in which women are made prominent by exclusion. All such passages combined form but one-tenth of the Scriptures, the undertaking will not be so laborious as, at the first thought, one would imagine. These texts, with the commentaries, can easily be compressed into a duodecimo volume of forty pages.

1. *Two or three Greek and Hebrew scholars will devote themselves to the translation and meaning of particular words in the original.*
2. *Others will devote themselves to Biblical history, old manuscripts, to the new version, and to take the latest theories as to the occult meaning of certain texts and parables.*
3. *For the commentaries in the plain English version a committee of some thirty members has been formed. These are women of earnestness and liberal ideas, quick to see the real purpose of the Bible as regards to their sex. Among them the various books of the Old and New Testaments will be distributed for comment.*

In her Introduction she states: *From the inauguration of the movement for woman's emancipation the Bible has been used to hold her in the "divinely endowed sphere," prescribed in the Old and New Testaments.*

The Civil War gave women more opportunities, especially in the North. For example, the Union Army's Sanitary Commission, organized regionally, was entirely composed of women—who raised an enormous amount of money for food, uniforms and medical supplies for Union soldiers. The Commission staffed Army hospitals, competed with men for Army contracts for the manufacture of military clothing, hired wives of volunteer soldiers to make uniforms, cared for families of drafted men, set up free 'hotels,' provided meals for soldiers in transport and guided wounded veterans back into civilian life. It demonstrated what women could do.

Women were involved in anti-slavery groups, as were many men. But women also became advocates of temperance groups—that is, outlawing liquor. Women's suffrage advocates began to emerge when they realized how powerless they were in their rights regarding children, divorce and the control of money.

In 1868 the Fourteenth and Fifteenth Amendments to the United States Constitution gave voting rights to former male slaves—specifically Black men. But not to women, white or of any color.

At the turn of the nineteenth century into the twentieth a variety of social changes came about so that women had access to more labor-saving devices. These innovations gave women more time to devote to issues that affected the home, and to educate themselves. Formal education was still denied to women.

It was socially unbecoming for a woman to speak in public, so they had no experience. But the Quakers, known as the Religious Society of Friends, allowed women to do so, considering everyone equal. Quakers believed that anyone could directly experience God through the person's inner light, rather than through ritual and ceremony. They believed that priests, ministers and rituals were not necessary. This experience was not limited by race, gender, or other factors.

As a result, many of the early women's suffrage movement speakers were Quakers, such as Susan B. Anthony. She was given a very hard time by audiences during the first few years of her speechmaking because she was a woman. And the fact that she wanted the vote for women was even worse.

Also in 1868, Sorosis was the first women's club for socialization and self-education founded by Jane Cunningham Croly. She called the members *the light seekers*. At that time women could not join professional organizations. They were for white males only, such as the New York Press Club, and many others. An example in Los Angeles was the Jonathan Club. Not until 1987 were women admitted as members. Rotary International in the United States did not admit women until 1989, but only because a U. S. Supreme Court ruling forced them to do so.

After one year the Sorosis club had eighty-three members which included six artists, twenty-three authors, six editors, one historian, eleven poets, nine teachers and lecturers, eight philanthropists, two physicians and four science writers.

Women in the clubs were encouraged to research whatever topic they were interested in, and then to verbally present a paper to the rest of the members. This was finally an opportunity for women to become experienced in the art of public speaking.

In 1889 there was a federation of 97 women's clubs in the United States with 61 of them sending delegates to a convention. In the California Federation Phoebe Apperson Hearst (the mother of William Randolph Hearst) was elected Treasurer, with Clara Burdette as 2nd Treasurer.

By 1890 the General Federation of Women's Clubs was organized, which brought together all the state federations of clubs.

The purpose of the clubs was self-education, with an agenda of music, art, history, geography, literature and a variety of topics *to enlarge their mental horizons.* Some clubs had a specific name such as Clio (the goddess of history), Shakespeare Society, Boston History Club, Castilian Club, Armchair Travelers, Ebell Club. The reason for the self-education was that major institutions of higher education were still not admitting women—and women wanted to learn. Yale didn't accept women until 1968.

When the clubs first started the papers presented at club meetings for the discussion did not include politics. There was definitely no talk of voting rights, as not all women felt the need to have the vote. The clubs did not want to alienate and lose members of this issue—yet.

The clubs gathered momentum with women's study clubs proliferating, meeting in each other's homes to study various subjects.

In 1876, Carolyn Severance—'the Mother of Clubs'—moved to Los Angeles and in 1891 founded the Friday Morning Club, which eventually built their own club house. The Friday Morning Club became very influential in itself, as well as a model for other clubs.

Severance wrote a play in which women were in charge and debated about giving men the vote. The dialog for one of the women is, *"If men were to vote, they would meddle in our affairs, they would all run into politics, the flour barrel would be empty...*" and she continued with examples of the woodhouse being empty of wood, and hinges falling off the doors because men would not be in their 'sphere' to fix things. A mirror image of what the men in charge had said.

In 1896—to show the tenor of the times—in Utah, the ladies' literary club had a successful first year. Church officials and others stated their concern and some members were severely censured. But that difficulty was removed when the officials attended a meeting and saw what the women were doing, all was well. The only change the men insisted on was that the meetings begin with a prayer.

In Colorado, Governor Alva Adams (Governor 1887-89, 1897-9, and 1905) welcomed a women's convention stating: *Women's sphere is no longer confined to the washtub, the kitchen, or the parlor. Her sphere is now the great whirling globe, with all the responsibilities and the glories. The growth of women's clubs is the greatest movement of this generation.* This was not a typical white male speech.

By 1900 the California Federation had 446 clubs with a membership of 76,459. Quite a remarkable increase. A shift in focus emerged as the clubs moved to legislative action. The Federation's first move was to secure passage of a law exempting the meadow lark as a game bird. The species was endangered. Later the women campaigned to save the redwoods, which were being decimated. Next, their actions were focused on a rehabilitation program for the women's prison at Tehachapi, and then a domiciliary home for women veterans at Yountville. They were drifting toward politics as were the other women's clubs in the country. And they had a slogan for that—Municipal Housekeeping.

The focus on self-education turned to education for the betterment of the community. What else could they do in that area? The women's club movement established the idea that women had a moral duty and responsibility to transform public policy. As mentioned above, the clubs started out as religious, then became social and literary gatherings, but soon became the source of reform for various issues. The clubs were also becoming training schools for women who wanted to get involved in the public sphere—beyond the home sphere. Because everything in politics affected the home—pure milk, sewage, tariffs—the list went on and on.

Debates on getting the vote for woman were not condoned by all clubwomen. Presidents of clubs and federations did not want to push the issue for fear of losing members. However, by 1900, clubs such as Wisconsin passed a suffrage resolution, but voting for women was limited to school elections only. The time had come, and the women realized that to make any civic changes, they needed legislation to do so. Women needed the vote to accomplish this.

In California because of the defeats of voting rights for women in 1893 and 1895, the women's suffrage movement went into the doldrums—as it was described. However, in 1905, the country's General Federation President Reverend Anna Howard Shaw, one of the first women to get an ecumenical degree, wrote to Mary McHenry Keith, a California attorney and a strong advocate for women's rights, stating: *Hold your clubs together by work not immediately pertaining to suffrage.* That turned out to be sterling advice.

In 1902 the California Federation of Women's Clubs encompassed 95 clubs with 7,000 members. In 1905, membership was 10,765. The Women's Temperance Union's membership which had always been the highest in the state, dropped significantly.

In Wisconsin in 1896, 103 delegates from 63 clubs formally organized into a state federation. Not until 1900 would the suffrage issue be voted on. But it was 'limited suffrage,' that is women should be allowed to vote on school matters. But it was a start on the political path.

In 1912, Jane Addams, co-founder of Hull House, one of the first settlement houses in North America, gave a stirring speech that resulted in an overwhelming vote for suffrage.

The General Federation convention met in 1912 with over 5,000 clubs represented. The movement kept growing.

Why is our time travel, our eagle eye survey of the states about women's clubs, important? Read on.

CHAPTER FOUR
CALIFORNIA 1894 AND 1896

The Chicago World's Fair, also titled the Columbian Exposition, in 1893 was considered the greatest one of the time period. Many Californian women attended—club women, temperance members, labor activists and suffragists—and women from throughout the country lobbied there for the vote.

It was called the Columbian Exposition because it celebrated the 400th anniversary of Christopher Columbus's landing on the continent. Forty-six countries had exhibits in the two hundred buildings set over six hundred acres, with canals and lagoons.

It far exceeded other world's fairs and lasted from May to October of 1893.

One of the buildings was designated for women where their achievements were exhibited. Plus, the World's Congress of Representative Women was a week-long convention for the voicing of women's concerns and was held in the Auxiliary building in conjunction with the Fair. American women organized eighty-one meetings with seventy-six sessions of speakers from around the world. One hundred and fifty thousand people attended and listened to speeches by almost five hundred women from twenty-seven countries. Two of the many noted speakers were Elizabeth Cady Stanton—"The Ethics of Suffrage," and Susan B. Anthony—"Organization Among Women as an Instrument in Promoting the Interest of Political Liberty."

It was the largest and most representative gathering of women from all over the women, beginning on May 15 and ending on May 21. The Conference reiterated that women throughout the world wanted the vote.

At that time in California the Populist or People's Party came into being because of several factors. The Party demanded federal regulation of railroad rates. The rates were at the whim of the railroad owners who could arbitrarily raise rates or cut service. The farmers needed the railroads to move their crops to market. Plus, the farmers wanted the government to establish federally controlled warehouses. Again, the owners could raise rates arbitrarily—and did.

The Party had several other measures that would prevent monopolies from taking advantage of anyone. These measures would also help small businesses, laborers and farmers. The Party was making inroads in the corrupt California political system and supported women's quest for the vote. Because the Party was becoming popular, the Republicans joined in supporting women getting the vote.

In 1893, the Temperance Union gathered 20,000 names for a petition to the California legislature on suffrage. The bill passed but the governor vetoed it. Then another bill was passed, granting suffrage—but only for voting in school elections. That bill was also vetoed by the governor.

In 1894, the Republican Party endorsed woman's suffrage, which they did again in 1910. The Democrats did not—and were highly opposed to the idea. The Democrats ruled California and change of any kind was not in their platform.

In 1895 Susan B. Anthony campaigned in California for the vote, and encouraged the movement to be non-partisan, that is, not support any Party but focus on the issues.

Then came November 3, 1896 and on the California ballot in the General Election was a Constitutional Amendment which would allow women to vote. It was #6 and was there through the efforts of the Temperance Union, suffrage organizations and women's clubs. Of the California voters, all male, less than 45% voted for it. So, it was defeated. The biggest losses were in San Mateo, Marin, Contra Costa, Sacramento and Sonoma counties—counties in the San Francisco area. The measure lost by 80,000 to 95,000. Both the *Los Angeles Times* and the *San Francisco Chronicle* were vehemently against anything to do with women getting the vote.

The large vote against mostly came from those who were afraid that women getting the vote would bring in prohibition against alcohol. It was a real concern that was rooted in economics. The alcohol industry was comprised of distilleries, breweries, wineries, saloons, restaurants, grocery stores, druggists (who filled prescriptions for alcohol), farmers who grew the products used, and all of the workers in all of these industries and establishments associated with alcohol, such as waitresses who would lose income if no alcohol was served in restaurants or hotels. To recent European immigrants, alcohol was a part of their culture.

The suffragists were composed largely of women who had enough income to be able to attend club meetings and push for the vote. The need to address working women, many in unions, was realized and those women became part of the suffrage movement.

CHAPTER FIVE
WHY CALIFORNIA WOMEN WANTED THE VOTE

The main argument in the woman's suffrage movement was taxation without representation. This was the slogan women threw back at the men that they had used against King George III and which started the American Revolution. Women were taxpayers but could not vote.

What else California women wanted:

1—raise the age of consent of a minor for girls from 16 to 18. For boys it was 21. This was the age at which individuals could marry without their parents' consent.

2—raise the minimum wage

3—extend laws to require an 8-hour day

4—establish a state training school for girls with a board of women trustees

5—ensure state teachers pensions

6—provide for equal guardianship of children. Currently, the father had sole guardianship which meant mothers were not allowed a say in their children's lives. Joint guardianship bills failed in 1909 and 1911.

7—implement no-fault divorce so that women could divorce their husbands. As it was, divorce was not allowed, even for extreme cruelty, adultery, willful desertion, willful neglect, habitual intemperance or conviction of a felony. Although divorce laws did come into effect, they were burdensome. No-fault divorce was not implemented until 1969.

8—hire women in the penal system. Women were arrested by men (no women police officers), tried by men (as no women were allowed on the jury), jailed and guarded by men (as there were no women matrons). Women wanted to change this by having women police officers and women matrons. Women being on juries was also a goal.

9—ensure juvenile justice reform, such as having separate facilities for children, as they were currently being jailed with adults

10—have female physicians in the women's wards and hospitals for the insane

11—provide for kindergarten and nursery schools, have smaller classroom size, provide safe playgrounds, and include art and music in the curriculum

12—allow women who married men of other nationalities to keep their own citizenship and not take on that of their husband unless the woman requested to do so

13—expand political decisions affecting the home—such as pure milk laws, lower tariffs on cloth so the price would come down, and laws on other items that affected the home and family.

14—promote a rehabilitation program at the women's prison at Tehachapi. The women wanted this for all women's prisons in the state.

15—create a domiciliary home for women veterans was needed at Yountville in Napa County

16—provide access to higher education for women, as almost no colleges and universities allowed the admittance of women

17—save the meadowlark from extinction

How could saving the meadowlark catapult California women into eventually getting the vote? In lobbying for legislation, women got an education as to how to accomplish what they wanted.

In the late 1800s women's hats became larger and more ornate and covered with feathers—from birds. Women must have been horrified to learn they were the prime users of feathers—and had been a party to the decimation of birds. Hummingbirds were especially vulnerable because of their iridescent feathers. Egrets, herons, ostriches, peacocks, grebes, terns and blackbirds were the most decimated. Not only the feathers but hats were decorated with wings, breasts, heads and bodies of entire stuffed birds.

The first bill was the 1901 Meadowlark Preservation Act which made it illegal to kill meadowlarks. In 1904 the California Audubon

Society, with a large contingent of women, was responsible for several conservation laws.

The Audubon Society was an environmental organization incorporated in the United States in 1905 but had been in existence before that. The organization was named for John James Audubon, a painter of birds, primarily and is known for his minute depiction of in his folios. The Birds of America contained colored plates of over one thousand birds.

In 1910 the California Legislature created Bird Day, which matched Arbor Day that was celebrated in public schools. Bird Day meant the children would learn the value of birds and the necessity of protecting them.

After getting the vote in 1911, California women continued their efforts in this area. In 1913 a bill was passed to protect thirty-eight species of shore birds, but Governor Hiram Johnson vetoed it, even though he said he was a conservationist. In 1915 a bill was passed that did the same job—the Protection of Wading Birds Act.

California Women and Politics states: Audubon women communicated with government representatives, arranged public speakers, circulated informational pamphlets to politicians and the general public, posted and vigorously enforced hunting regulations in their communities, and attempted in other ways to educate the public about local and statewide protective laws won through their exhaustive lobbying efforts.

California women also wrote popular literature about birds, initiated education programs in schools, and organized Junior Audubon clubs to ensure that future generations would be knowledgeable about and sympathetic to bird protections.

Women who were part of clubs used their networks—and their organizing skills—to give a wakeup call to the complacent male policymakers and businessmen.

Next on the list:

18—save the redwoods from extinction. In both cases—the meadowlarks and the redwoods— women authored the legislation. Each group had women attorneys, as well as access to husbands, brothers and fathers who were attorneys. The women also lobbied their representatives.

But the early 20th century awakened to the natural resources that were being wasted. Birds, species of which couldn't be replaced, were decimated. The redwood trees were hundreds of years old, unique in that they only grew in a certain climate—and when they were gone, they were gone.

Women's clubs had other projects—but these two projects—save the meadowlark and redwoods—showed how influential they could be—if organized. Different groups worked together and formed alliances—specifically with like-minded men—to achieve their goals.

19—strengthen the red light abatement act. Women's organizations saw the need for better communities and campaigned for what they wanted accomplished. One of the items was abatement of red light districts where prostitution was controlled. The red light districts were rampant with crimes that spilled over into the adjacent communities.

The women deluged their legislators with letters and telegrams in support of a vote for the red-light abatement bill. It made an impact and many legislators saw the women's organizations as a voting bloc, which they were at that time—and which could be to the legislators' benefit. Or if they did not support these issues, then the future of the legislators might be precarious. One senator said that he felt pressured by his constituents to vote for it.

The war on prostitution was waged through a publicity campaign and legislative networking. It was noted that the steady, intelligent, cooperative pressure of the women on their representatives forced the latter to do something.

The Red Light Abatement Act went on the ballot, which meant another campaign for women's organizations. There was a lot more to the story, and lots of machinations, but the point is—the women were organized and unrelenting.

Birds, trees and red light districts had not been on any of the male legislators' agendas.

20—create a pure milk law was another issue that was considered to be in the women's purview and not necessarily one that a male politician would think of. Centering on the domestic front, women were concerned with the anti-tuberculosis pure milk issue. Milk that they bought was not being pasteurized so that tubular infection from the cows was being passed on to children when they drank it.

21—improve sanitation and living conditions in cities. Because women made up half of the population, their property ownership could not be ignored. Women who owned property made their voices known about how the area in which they lived was governed. Also, they wanted parks, churches, schools, and other amenities that added to the betterment of the community. On their list of improvements was better sanitation, purer water, garbage collection, sewers and other amenities that we take for granted today.

Women needed the vote, which would give them the right to participate in society. What the women needed was equality under the law, property rights, guardianship of their children, and access to education—the same as men had.

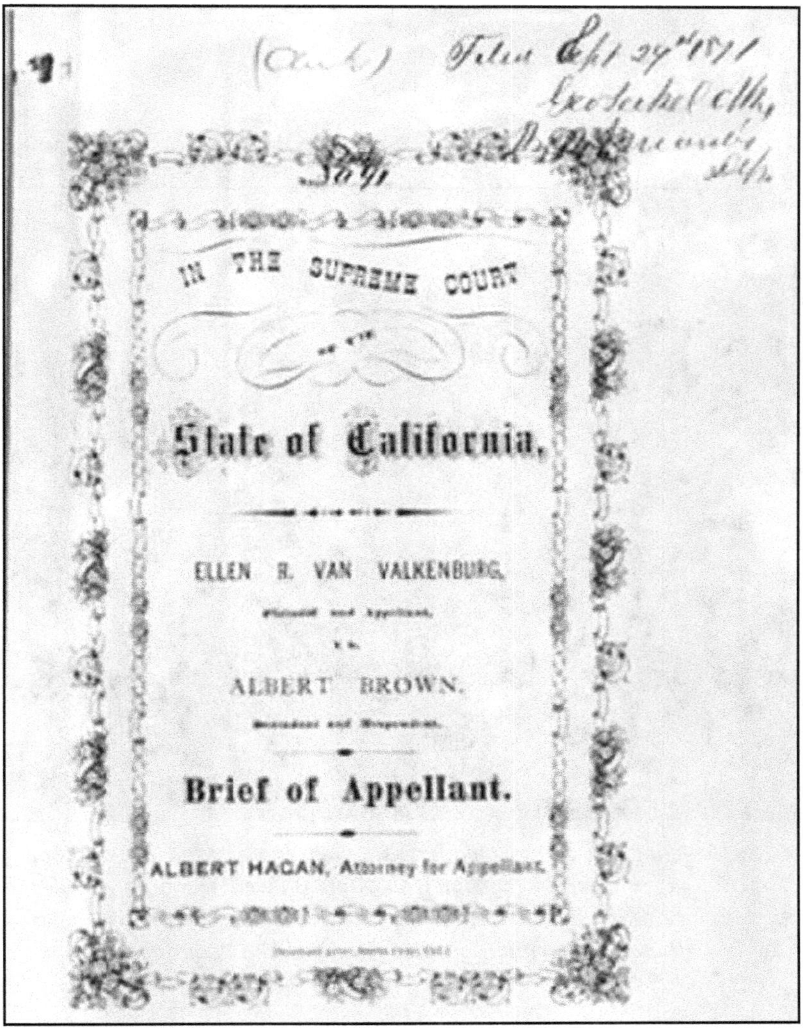

IN THE SUPREME COURT

State of California.

ELLEN R. VAN VALKENBURG,

vs.

ALBERT BROWN,

Brief of Appellant.

ALBERT HAGAN, Attorney for Appellant.

Ellen Van Valkenburg filed this brief in 1871 in Santa Cruz after she was denied the right to vote because she was a woman.
Photo: https://www.sos.ca.gov/archives/women-get-right-vote/women-get-right-vote-selected-documents/

1896 meeting of Suffragist leaders: standing (l to r) Ida Husted Harper, Selena Solomons, Carrie Chapman Catt, Anne Bidwell, (seated) Lucy Anthony, Dr. Anna H. Shaw, Susan B. Anthony, Ellen Clark Sargent, and Mary Hay. Photo: California Historical Society, San Francisco, CA

Organizers of the 1911 Amendment 8 campaign gathered in San Francisco for a publicity shot.
Photo: Women Voting Throughout the Years

The Yellow Ribbon

DEVOTED TO THE INTERESTS OF WOMAN SUFFRAGE ON THE PACIFIC COAST

Volume 1 | SAN FRANCISCO, OCTOBER, 1909 | Number 1

PROGRESS OF EQUAL SUFFRAGE IN CALIFORNIA

MARY SIMPSON SPERRY

REASONS WHY WOMEN SHOULD HAVE A VOTE

MRS. MARY S. SPERRY,
President California Equal Suffrage Association.

The Yellow Ribbon, October 1909.

Woman's Party Booth at San Francisco Exposition Spring 1915.
L-R, Front - 1 Mrs. May Wright Sewall, 2 Mrs. Kate Waller Barrett (Alexandria, Va), Rear - 3 Miss Anita Whitney (Cal.), 4 Mrs. Mary Beard, 5 Miss Vivian Pierce, 6 Miss Margaret Whittemore.
Photo: Library of Congress, Records of the National Woman's Party.

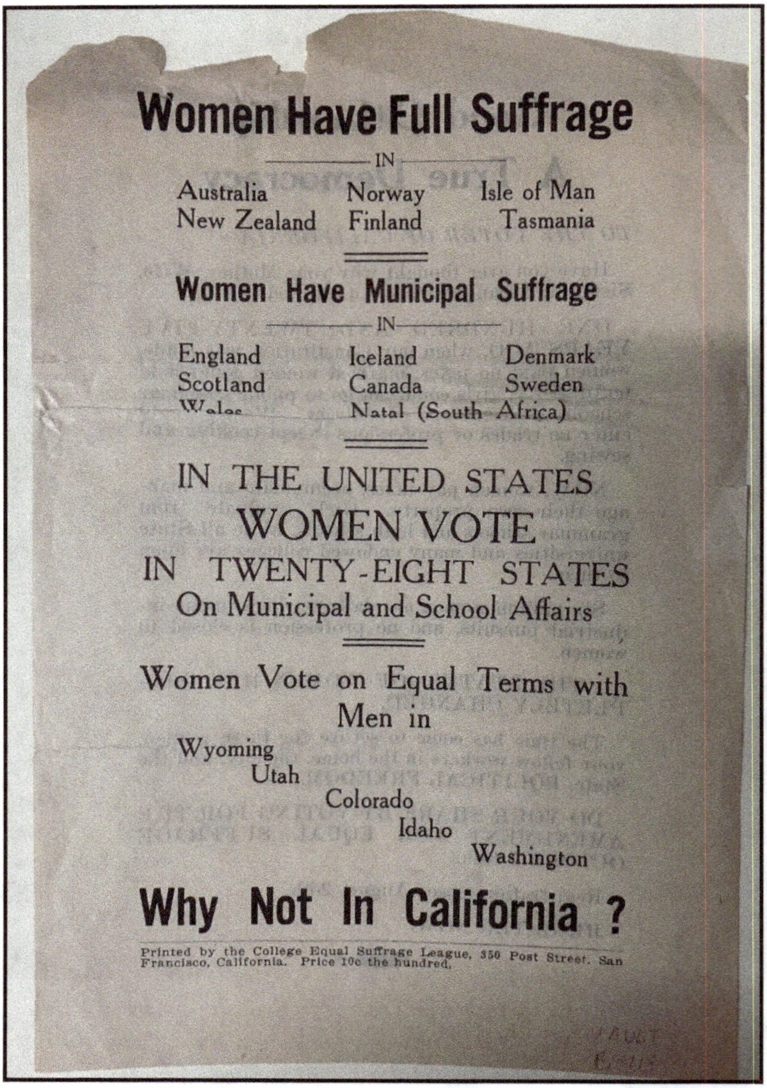

Poster: Women have full suffrage in Australia, New Zealand, Norway, Finland, Isle of Man, Tasmania... Why not in California? Printed by the College Equal Suffrage League, ca. 1911, San Francisco. California Historical Society, Vault B-119.

Women's Voter Convention, San Francisco, 1915. Alva Belmont seated second from right.
Photo: Library of Congress, National Woman's Party Records,

"Votes for Women" "California Next," 1910 NAWSA postcard campaign.
Photo: National Museum of American History

Photograph of National Woman's Party members seated in and speaking from a car on a street crowded with people. Speakers wear prison dresses, one holds a suffrage flag, 1911.
Photo: Library of Congress, Records of the National Woman's Party.

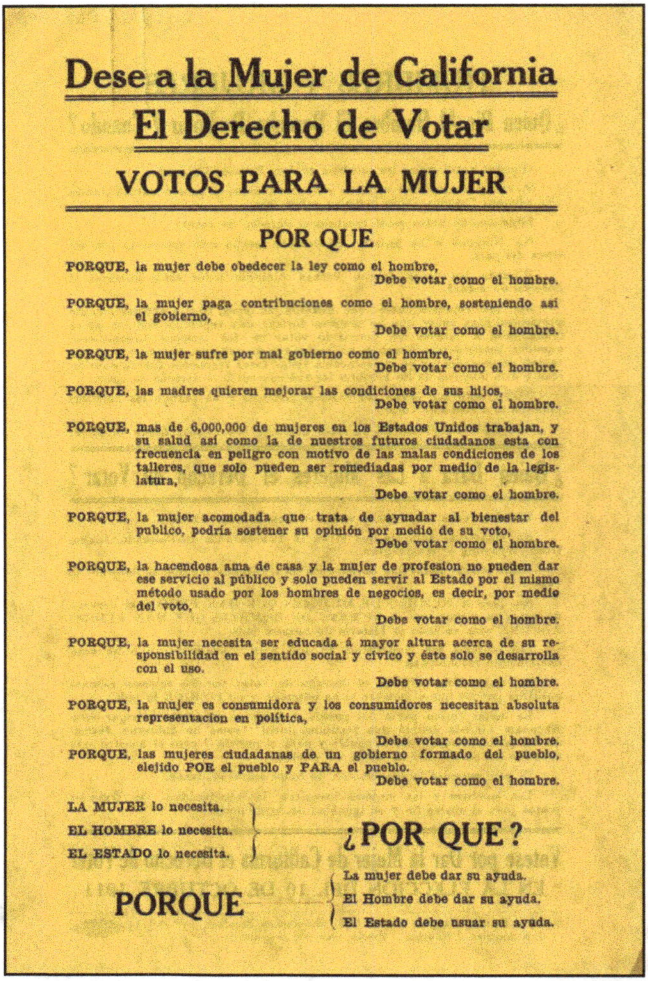

Dese a la Mujer de California El Derecho de Votar

VOTOS PARA LA MUJER

POR QUE

PORQUE, la mujer debe obedecer la ley como el hombre,
Debe votar como el hombre.

PORQUE, la mujer paga contribuciones como el hombre, sosteniendo asi el gobierno,
Debe votar como el hombre.

PORQUE, la mujer sufre por mal gobierno como el hombre,
Debe votar como el hombre.

PORQUE, las madres quieren mejorar las condiciones de sus hijos,
Debe votar como el hombre.

PORQUE, mas de 6,000,000 de mujeres en los Estados Unidos trabajan, y su salud asi como la de nuestros futuros ciudadanos esta con frecuencia en peligro con motivo de las malas condiciones de los talleres, que solo pueden ser remediadas por medio de la legislatura,
Debe votar como el hombre.

PORQUE, la mujer acomodada que trata de ayudar al bienestar del publico, podría sostener su opinión por medio de su voto,
Debe votar como el hombre.

PORQUE, la hacendosa ama de casa y la mujer de profesion no pueden dar ese servicio al público y solo pueden servir al Estado por el mismo método usado por los hombres de negocios, es decir, por medio del voto,
Debe votar como el hombre.

PORQUE, la mujer necesita ser educada á mayor altura acerca de su responsibilidad en el sentido social y cívico y éste solo se desarrolla con el uso.
Debe votar como el hombre.

PORQUE, la mujer es consumidora y los consumidores necesitan absoluta representacion en política,
Debe votar como el hombre.

PORQUE, las mujeres ciudadanas de un gobierno formado del pueblo, elejido **POR** el pueblo y **PARA** el pueblo.
Debe votar como el hombre.

LA MUJER lo necesita.
EL HOMBRE lo necesita.
EL ESTADO lo necesita.

¿POR QUE?

PORQUE

La mujer debe dar su ayuda.
El Hombre debe dar su ayuda.
El Estado debe usuar su ayuda.

Pamphlet of the Los Angeles Political Equality League by Maria de Lopez. Pamphlet that was translated to Spanish during suffrage movement. Photo: Women's Suffrage and Equal Rights Collection, Ella Strong Denison Library, Scripps College, Claremont, California. Los Angeles Political Equality League.

Women Voters Frisco – Registering shop girls & clerks.
Photo: Library of Congress, Bain News Service, publisher.

How We Won the Vote in California: A true story of the campaign of 1911 by Selina Solomons. Publication date 1912. Women, Suffrage Publisher San Francisco, California.
Photo: https://archive.org/details/howwewonvoteinca00solo/page/n3/mode/2up?ref=ol&view=theater. The New Woman Publishing Co. Collection

Clara Elizabeth Chan Lee (October 21, 1886 – October 5, 1993) was the first Chinese American woman to register to vote in the United States. Photo: Oakland Tribune November 8, 1911. https://localwiki.org/oakland/Clara_Elizabeth_Chan_Lee/_files/Clara%20Lee.jpg/_info/

First woman jury, Los Angeles, 1911.
Photo: Library of Congress, Bain News Service photograph collection.

CHAPTER SIX
WHAT CHANGED BY 1911?

1 **Temperance**. The suffragists separated their cause from the Temperance Union, although many were members of both. The Temperance Union favored outlawing liquor. Too many husbands came home drunk having spent their wages at one of the many saloons. This left many families destitute.

After 1881 the Union joined with the suffragists and expanded its mission—and that coincided with the woman's suffrage movement issues—prisons, eight-hour work day, women's vocational education, child labor abolishment, kindergartens, and boardinghouses for women.

The amalgamation was a significant boost to the rolls of the suffragist movement. The first Temperance chapter was formed in 1878 in California. In 1879 six chapters had about two hundred members, then ten years later there were 3,687 members, with 117 chapters in the north and 1,481 members in the south. Most members were potential suffragists.

The problem in being aligned with the Temperance Union was that beer, wine and spirits were part of the culture of immigrant and working-class communities. Hotels and restaurants served liquor where bartenders, waiters and waitresses worked, as well as other industries involving liquor.

Plus, many people made their living brewing, fermenting, distilling, transporting and selling liquor. Germans, Irish and Italians made up a large part of the immigrant population in San Francisco and they were the ones primarily involved in the liquor industry. And the men were voters. The liquor industry spent a lot of money to thwart women from getting the vote.

The saloon was often a male social and political center—just as English pubs were. The many saloons offered card games, billiards, gambling machines, as well as free or cheap lunches. There, ward heelers—men who worked for a political party to make sure the voters voted 'correctly'—contacted the men in their precincts. Unions held meetings there. Voting was done in many saloons where a drink was offered for a vote.

The June 1, 1893 issue of the *Pacific Ensign,* the California newspaper of the Women's Temperance Union, acknowledged that women getting the vote just might solve a lot of problems. The California branch was the largest in the country at that time. *Woman is everywhere the purifier as she makes brighter and purer the home life, so will she elevate and cleanse the moral atmosphere of State and nation. In the crusade against wrong her hour has come.*

2 **Polling Places.** Men voted in saloons, livery stables, barber shops—places where men congregated. That would change to schools, libraries, churches and other venues that were acceptable for women to enter—when women got the right to vote.

3 **Automobiles.** In 1893 moving around the state relied on horse and buggy or the railroad. Travel was a slow process. By 1911 women were able to travel to remote areas in a car. True, there were difficulties—breakdowns, no roads or ones that weren't much more than muddy tracks, lack of service and gas stations,

The cars had soft or convertible-type tops so that women could stand up on a seat or a platform in the car and use the car as a podium. Stop anywhere where people might gather and start talking, standing up in the car, such as on the back seat. No need to hire a hall or place to speak.

4 **Politics**. The Political Party in Sacramento had changed. The Party in power in 1893 was, as rumor had it, in the pockets of the railroads which had a lot of money thanks to the United States government which wanted railroads built—and fast. Money in the pockets of the railroad men meant that some could bribe the California legislators, if the elected man wanted to participate in such a transaction. Whether that was true or not, it was the rumor. But in 1893 there was a Depression, which caused one quarter of the nation's railroads to go bankrupt. Massive layoffs followed. This lessened the power of the railroads drastically. The

automobile would have a great impact on continuing the demise of the railroads.

The Political Parties now in power in California were the Progressives, and the Socialists. Both wanted corruption, graft and similar items out of politics. The Socialists had always taught and stood for the complete emancipation of women—socially, economically and politically. Both Parties wanted progress. This meant they were much more amenable to 'giving' women the vote.

5 **Education and working women.** In the early twentieth century more women pursued higher education—and more women held jobs outside the home. Plus, there were reliable methods of birth control—but no pill yet.

In the early 1900s, the San Francisco working women began to unionize. Mostly, they had strong support from the men. By 1910, six percent of working women—that is, those earning wages, were members of unions, many predominately female ones. In comparison nationwide—only1.5 percent of working women were in unions.

In 1911 San Francisco was an immigrant Catholic town containing a sizable working class population. Susan Englander in her book *Class Coalition* states that of the second-generation residents and the largest population of which one-quarter were Irish, with Germans second and then Italians. Women were 43% of the population, comprising 18.4% of the city labor force. One-third of all employed women were Irish. Those statistics for women broke down to one-third servants and waitresses, one-third laundry workers and one-third were teachers. Women members of the union were 1100 laundry workers, 536 waitresses, and 500 garment workers.

The labor vote was crucial as it could help or hinder the passage of a California constitutional amendment.

6 **Social conditions.** Customs and mores had changed considerably from 1893. Women speaking to groups, or crowds, or even joining organizations other than those church-related, was not as shocking. And women going out into the world was not frowned upon as it had been.

7 **Labor-saving devices.** No more did women have to spin to make fabric and sew to make clothes for themselves and their families. Ready-to-wear garments were available. Hot and cold water came out of a tap, not pulled up from a well, then heated on the stove. No more bread making, canning fruits and vegetables or butter-churning. All could be bought from a store.

Flexner states in her *Century of Struggle* other innovations—the development of gas lighting, municipal water systems, indoor plumbing, canning of foods, the production of ice, improvements in furnaces and stoves, and the invention of the sewing machine. All of these provided an escape from the drudgery of housekeeping. Also, as mentioned above, California had more immigrants who were willing to be cooks and nursemaids.

8 **Political issues.** These affected the home. Issues that women wanted to address had meaning in every home. High tariffs on items needed in the home meant higher prices and scarcity of these items. Women wanted anti-tuberculosis pure milk, child labor laws, minimum-wage and maximum-hours for workers, childcare centers, parks and playgrounds, pure food and drug laws, clean city water systems, garbage collection, libraries, juvenile justice reform, female physicians in women's wards and hospitals for the insane. The women wanted to better the community where they and their children lived.

9 **Legal issues.** These included women's property rights, marital status, control of children's lives—all of which were not in women's favor. Since the laws favored men, those political issues had not been addressed.

10 **Higher education.** More women were going on for degrees in various professions. No longer were the sons of the family the only ones who were educated. The cry before had been—why does a woman need education to stay home and keep house and have and raise children. Now, more women held jobs outside the home. Women wanted to be doctors, lawyers, professors, meaning access to higher education to achieve their goals.

11 **Women's clubs.** Since 1893, in particular, more women's clubs had been organized. They started not as political clubs but to learn more about the world they lived in—science, the arts, history. Not only were women's clubs formed in each town, but each state had a federation of all of the clubs in the state, and the United States had a General Federation of clubs from all of the states. It was quite a network. And the suffragists used this network. Yes, there were members who were antis—those against women getting the vote—but the majority ruled. The majority wanted the vote.

12 **Rights.** Women realized early on that having the vote meant they had rights—rights to property, and other human rights. Plus, rights gave them power to make changes in the laws—and even to oust those who represented them.

13 **Organized religion.** The all-male clergy were against women stepping out of their sphere—namely the home. The home was where they were expected to have and care for children and devote their lives to the happiness and comfort of their husbands. No consideration was given to what the women wanted for happiness. The clergy wanted to keep that status quo—, which meant keeping women in their 'sphere.'

The start of this 'rebellion' by women went back to the early 1800s with the anti-slavery movement, such as the Grimke sisters—Angelina and Sara, and later Lucy Stone. (She married Henry S. Blackwell but kept her name and was known as Mrs. Stone.) She and others, including Blackwell, followed William Lloyd Garrison who chastised the churches—all of them—for supporting slavery, or for not coming out against it. The Garrisonians were considered to be heathens, pagans, and whatever else they could be called, but their only objection to churches was that organized religion did not take a stand against slavery.

Many anti-slavery advocates agreed. Infallibility and the position of organized religion was questioned by the Garrisonians and others.

There was a correlation between slavery and the 'sphere' to which women were relegated.

14 **Monied women.** Women in higher income brackets, through their husband, father or themselves, could pay others to do work in the home. The high immigration of women helped to supply the workforce to fill this need. Therefore, the wealthier women had more time to devote to doing good in the community. The latter was influenced by women's clubs. And with the vote they could do more.

15 **Working women.** More women were working outside of the home and they needed better working conditions, higher pay, and benefits such as vacations and health care. Unions helped to force the issues and achieved some of these goals.

Because the workforce of women expanded, the suffragists realized that they needed to recruit working women. The campaign to get the vote needed the help of working women—and in turn, achieving that goal would benefit all.

16 **Telephones.** By 1890, 1% of American households had a phone, with more in commercial establishments. This type of communication was immensely helpful during the 1911 campaign for the vote by California women. It meant instant communication with all parts of the large state.

17 **Quakers.** The Quaker religion had a tradition of public service. Many of those in the suffragist movement were Quakers. As mentioned earlier, the Quakers believed that all people were equal—and women were speakers at their meetings. That meant the Quaker women had the confidence and experience in talking before groups. And many Quaker women were suffragists.

18 **Heads of Households.** More women holding jobs outside of the home were the main supporters of their families. The United States Census of 1900 reported that over 14 million women were the breadwinners for their families, or even just for themselves. This meant they were as concerned as other women about laws that affected the home—and laws that were not on the books yet.

In 1906 the California newspaper the *Oakland Enquirer* stated that *women have a right to support and to make a career for themselves are no longer debatable questions.* This was quite a statement when society expected a woman to go from being cared for by her father, who handed her over to being cared for by a husband.

Her choice role was that of the Victorian angel of the house; soothing, ministering, arranging, placating…interviewing servants, dealt with business matters, typed manuscripts and checked proofs, was the comment of Jane, the wife of H. G. Wells, a famous author in England. The point being that the woman only existed to serve others.

19 **Unions**. The Wage Earners' Suffrage League, shortened to WESL, was formed in 1908 to advocate and win better conditions for working women and to promote suffrage. The women who formed it attended the National Woman's Trade Union League Convention. This organization became an important part of the suffrage movement.

20 **Fashions**. The puffy sleeves, dress train and the hour-glass figure were out. Corsets no longer gave the woman a derriere and a pigeon breast. Elaborate hair pieces and hats were not the style in 1910. Women had more freedom of movement than previously. In 1909, the overall look was a straighter line, less formal and with less material. Hats were simpler—no more bird feathers—and clothing became more comfortable, durable and functional.

21 **Voter Education.** To counteract the accusation that women didn't know how to vote, political education was introduced into the suffragist organizations. That led to the founding of the League of Women Voters.

22 **Issues**. The suffragist movement adopted the goal of making whatever party was in power accountable for not granting women the right to vote. And, like their English sisters, the women encouraged people not to vote for those candidates or party.

FROM 1896 TO 1911

In summary, much had changed.

In 1894 and 1896, the referendum which would give women the vote in California was defeated mostly by the liquor industry that frightened those who did not want prohibition of alcohol. It was a scare tactic and it worked. Suffragism was too much entwined with the Temperance movement at the time.

By 1910 more women were educated. Women's clubs became more educated in the field of politics and the backgrounds of the candidates, learned about the issues and how to get laws passed, specifically those that benefited their families.

The focus of the women was not on the candidate or the party but on the cause. Women were more interested in causes than Party affiliation or specific candidates. They got behind measures important for the welfare of women and children. The legislators heard from their home district which bills to support. Would they do the right thing? If not, they'd have a problem.

HOW THE MEASURE GOT ON THE BALLOT: CALIFORNIA LEGISLATURE 1911

Maud Younger argued in "The Wage Earners' Need for the Ballot"—that working women needed the vote. Younger testified at the hearings on the amendment, facing a group of anti-suffragists. The resolution passed in the California Senate and the Assembly. It went on the ballot on February 2, 1911, one of 23 amendments to the California Constitution, to be voted on by male Californians in a special election on October 10, 1911.

CHAPTER SEVEN
HOW THE SUFFRAGISTS GOT THE MEASURE ON THE BALLOT

Because of the network of women's clubs, the suffrage organizers were able to appoint a chairwoman in each county, and one in each city and town. This network helped when the women traveled around to speak. The network provided food, shelter, contacts and arrangements for venues or halls where they could speak to larger audiences.

Considerable animosity existed against the 1911 speakers—not because they were women speaking—but because they were trying to get the vote for women. Having the network helped to quell some of the more vocal people—men, women and boys—from too much of a display of their animosity.

Dedicated women worked just as hard against obtaining the vote, as noted in the first chapter. But there were also a lot of men supporting women getting the vote.

When the all-male California Legislature voted against woman suffrage earlier, the movement had to regroup and find a new strategy.

Some politicians responded to the groups that tried to improve the environment and society. The women had become increasingly sophisticated in their efforts to get media attention, circulated petitions, had letter-writing campaigns, did personal lobbying, and educated the public about the issues.

There was nothing threatening in their issues that raised people's ire. The issues could be used to male politicians' advantage. Politicians recognized the value of issues that could be considered to be in the women's sphere of interest—not ones that men would initiate. They could be seen as 'good guys'—a win-win situation. Mainstream values were what the women pursued, and they were using the 'domestic approach' to the issue, that is, couching them in terms of home and hearth—'Municipal Housekeeping'—was the slogan.

Yet the logging companies did not appreciate not being able to cut down the giant redwood trees. The industry provided jobs a chain of jobs—for example, loggers, furniture-makers, sales people. The industry had lobbyists, too. But the overall good for society and the environment overcame that. Now there would be new jobs in conservation, tourism and related professions and industries.

Theda Skocpol, an American sociologist and political scientist, called this kind of activism done by women as *maternalism*. A term that meant women were not trying to participate in the patronage-driven male political world which had existed and was still the norm.

In January 1911 California suffrage officials made their biannual trip to Sacramento. What changed in the legislature to the advantage of the suffrage movement was that the reformed Lincoln-Roosevelt League dominated the Republication Party. The logjam of the control that the Southern Pacific Railroad machine had on the legislature was now broken. New primaries were held in the summer of 1910.

The Progressives were on the Republican Party Platform Committee to help write the Party's platform for the upcoming election. They were also now in the legislature. Governor Hiram Johnson was one of them. However, he was not an ardent supporter of suffragism, but he was also not totally adamant against it.

As a result, the Platform included a plank recommending that a constitutional amendment giving women the vote be put to a public referendum. That meant that it would be on the California ballot for—Californians to vote on. That had been the goal of the suffragists—getting women's suffrage as one of the planks of all of the Political Parties.

The Republicans were for it. The Democrats were on the other side of the fence as they had always been.

Proposition 4 was Senate Constitutional Amendment No. 8 that granted women the right to vote in the state for the first time. It was adopted by the California State Legislature and put on the ballot as part of a special election.

The ballot measure read:

TITLE [Rights of Suffrage (Permitting Women to Vote).]

Prop. No. 4 1911 General Election Summary [Rights of Suffrage (Permitting Women to Vote).] 4. SENATE CONSTITUTIONAL AMENDMENT NO. 8. CHAPTER 16. - Senate Constitutional Amendment No. 8, a resolution to propose to the people of the State of California an amendment to section one of article two of the constitution relating to the rights of suffrage.

Proposition type: Senate Constitutional Amendment Text of Proposition: The legislature of the State of California, at its regular session commencing on the second day of January, nineteen hundred and eleven, two thirds of the members elected in each of the two houses of the said legislature voting in favor thereof, hereby proposes the section one of article two of the constitution of the State of California be amended:

A "yes" vote supports this state constitutional amendment to provide women with the right to vote.

A "no" vote opposes this state constitutional amendment to provide women with the right to vote.

CHAPTER EIGHT
SLOGANS AND OTHER PUBLICITY

For the long work day,

For the taxes we pay,

For the laws we obey,

We want something to say!

Give the women a Square Deal on Oct. 10

The hand that rocks the cradle rears the patriot.

Votes for Women

Because

Women are citizens of a government of the people,

By the people and for the people

And women are people.

Women ought to GIVE their help

Men ought to HAVE their help

The State ought to USE their help.

Men their rights and nothing more,

Women their rights and nothing less

If politics is in baby food

Why should not mother be in politics?

MAN: Who is going to rock the cradle when mother goes off to vote?

MOTHER: The same person who rocks the cradle when mother goes off to pay her taxes!

These slogans and others with pleas to vote for the amendment approval were on posters, calendars, playing cards and every other word-bearing item. In San Francisco the words were on trolley cars—and everywhere on passenger cars in California.

No TV, internet or other means of spreading the word existed. Newspapers were the primary source of publicity at the time. Most of the large newspapers printed editorials, letters and articles from the suffragists. Seven hundred newspapers were being published in California at the time—and the women had a network to take advantage of this publicity opportunity.

The women used the printed newspaper articles in leaflets, posters, signs, shopping bags, billboards, electric signs and others which were placed in store and office window, ballparks, the ferry dock—and even duck blinds in the San Francisco Bay. Essay contests in schools, special plays and pageantry, lantern slides in nickelodeons and theaters further spread the plea to vote for the suffrage amendment. In small towns, parlor talks, and countless small meetings were held. Even a suffrage doll was available for the children. All means of publicity barraged the voting men.

In San Francisco, a seven-passenger touring car brought speakers, decorations and supplies to and from meetings. The suffragists spent a lot of time and effort in rural areas having learned from their previous campaigns in 1894 and 1896. As it turned out—those votes counted.

Ninety thousand *Votes for Women* buttons and three million pages of literature were distributed. Banners, posters, stickers, postcards, leaflets, stationery and other campaign items were simple but had striking designs, colors and text. The California Federation of Women's Clubs had 25,000 members, many of whom participated in the 1911 campaign.

Testimonials and endorsements by national leaders, prominent residents of the western equal suffrage states and labor leaders were publicized. Catholic priests were finally released by the bishop to express their own opinion. Leaflets titled "Extracts from the Speech of Father Gleason," which expressed his support of the vote, were distributed.

Publicity targeted the urban working class and racial ethnic voters through the foreign languages' newspapers, churches, social organizations and trade unions. Greek, Portuguese, French, German, Swedish and other languages including Mandarin were all used on publicity flyers and pamphlets. Labor suffragists were considered essential for the working-class support.

Every legitimate method of campaigning was used, beginning with the printing of 900,000 leaflets...posters and all kinds of designs; city circularizing of the most thorough kind in many languages; pageants, plays, concerts and public social functions; the placarding of city billboards over miles of county...huge electric and other signs; long weeks of automobile campaigning in the country and the villages; special speakers; a handsome float in the labor day parade; speaking at vaudeville shows.

And about that float in San Francisco—

This opportunity to visualize before tens of thousands of people the need of the working woman for the vote, was one not to let slip. As a team of prize-winning black horses wearing yellow livery pulled the float down Market Street, large banners announcing the suffrage message floated from each corner. There were two tableaux: on a higher, smaller platform were two allegorical female figures representing California asking Justice for the ballot, while the lower level consisted of real working women engaged in their representative tasks. Shop clerks, a typist, sewing and cannery workers, a nurse, and a professional woman in cap and gown joined a mother surrounded by young children. The float bore the slogan—These women need the ballot—while the children held a sign that read "Give our mother a vote."

Caricatures of cute children were used in many of the publicity items. Of course they were asking for the vote for their mother.

Catholic suffragists targeted the heavily Catholic working class by leafleting all thirty-six Catholic churches in San Francisco. They were at the doors of the churches at the early mass—six o'clock in the morning—and all the other services.

Registration booths were set up in department stores, banks and churches. Members went door- to-door, held afternoon teas and picnics. Noon talks were set up for the working women. Five thousand American flags were given away.

On election day over four hundred automobiles were available, covered in red, white and blue, to be for the get-out-the-vote campaign and to ferry voters to the polls.

CHAPTER NINE
GOAL TO BE THE SIXTH STAR

California would be the sixth star in the suffragist flag of those states where women had the right to vote. So far there were stars for Colorado, Utah, Idaho, Washington and Wyoming. That meant that all the women in those states could vote for the President—but the women in other states could not.

Wyoming had wanted more women settlers—it had an overabundance of men—so by giving them the vote the state was able to attract women.

Utah wanted to strengthen the political power of the Mormons and could do that by giving the women of polygamist marriages the vote.

Washington State had voted 2-1 for suffrage.

None of these situations existed in California.

But to make an impact on the nation and the suffrage movement, the suffragists needed a big win—a big state. The push for California to vote for suffrage was as important on the national level as it was on the state level.

Even though times had changed, how much would it affect the voters in California?

A cliffhanger, to be sure. The win came down to a close margin. The "yes" vote won by 50.73% with 125,037 votes. The "no" vote received 49.27% with 121,450 votes.

A reflection on how close the vote was. Remember, only males could vote. And there were a lot of antis out there—women and men who didn't want women to have the vote.

More cliffhangers were to come.

On Oct 2, 1911, the amendment to the California State Constitution granted women the right to vote. That meant they could vote in the

November election for the President of the United States. Heady stuff after years of trying to get the right that should have been theirs when the men got theirs.

CHAPTER TEN
DENOUEMENT

Now to get the United States House and Senate to pass the amendment.

In 1915, the Congressional Union for Women Suffrage sponsored an automobile ride across the country to take a petition with signatures to the President. The signatures were gathered at the Freedom Booth of the Panama Pacific International Exposition in San Francisco. The many signatures took up a lot of paper—18,000 feet long. The women drove the gigantic roll in their car. Of course, the women used the trip to gather more signatures, as each suffragist club on their stops held parades, autocades, meetings and rallies. After three months, they decided to ship the roll, but it was lost in transit from Wilmington, Delaware to Washington, D.C. But they had a back-up roll, although it was not as long, therefore not as impressive. In D.C. they were met by 1000 suffragists and paraded to the Capitol to present the petition to Congress.

The act in itself was crowd-drawing, as very few women drove cars/ Plus there were not a lot of cars on the road. Driving in those days was a challenge because roads were fine for horse and buggy but not for cars.

The car became a symbol of the woman suffrage movement. It also revealed the 'new woman' who could fend for herself.

President Wilson promised to 'keep an open mind,' which he did for too long. He refused to ask the Democratic Party to back the amendment. He was not a supporter of women's rights.

The Susan B. Anthony amendment was passed in the House on May 21, 1919—then on June 4, 1919, it passed in the Senate by a narrow margin but over the required two-thirds votes.

> *The right of citizens of the United States to vote shall not be denied or abridged by the United States or by any State on account of sex.*
>
> *Congress shall have power to enforce this article by appropriate legislation.*

It only took forty-one years from when it was first introduced in 1878 by California Senator Aaron A. Sargent.

A touch of irony was that President Wilson had a debilitating stroke on October 2, 1919, shortly after the amendment passed.

The right of women to vote was achieved in 1920. Next on the women's agenda was the constitutional amendment to guarantee equality.

Ratification by two thirds of all of the states was another cliffhanger.

The amendment needed two-thirds of the states to ratify it. Most of the state legislatures were off for the summer. The women wanted to be able to vote in November for the election of the president who would take office in 1920. They approached governors to help. Wisconsin was the first to ratify the amendment on June 10, 1919.

The women campaigned tirelessly to have thirty-six of the forty-eight states ratify the amendment. (Hawaii and Alaska were not states at the time.)

The ordeal was stranger than fiction, coming down to one vote in the Tennessee legislature, the last state to vote.

On August 18, 1920, the 36th state—Tennessee ratified the amendment 50-49. That meant that three-fourths of all of the states had passed it. The amendment was ratified on August 18, 1920. Most states allowed the women to register to vote in the presidential election in November—but some states did not work to speed up the registration process.

In 1920 over 8 million women had the right to vote.

BIBLIOGRAPHY

Note: General Bibliography items are available in most libraries. The Huntington items are only available to registered scholars for use in the library.

GENERAL BIBLIOGRAPHY

Adams, Jad. *Pankhurst*. Hau Publishing 2003

Ashby, LeRoy. *The Spearless Leader: Senator Borah and the Progressive Movement in the 1920s.* University of Illinois Press 1972

Blackwell, Alice Stone. *Lucy Stone.* Little, Brown and Company 1930

Blair, Karen J. *The Clubwoman as Feminist.* Holes & Meier Pub 1980. [rare book purchased]

Burdette, Clara Bradley. *The Answer to "Clara, what are you going to do with your life?"* The Clara Vista Press 1951

— *The Rainbow and the Pot of Gold.* The Clara Vista Press 1908

Club Women of California

Cherny, Robert W., Mary Ann Irwin, Ann Marie Wilson, editors. *California Women and Politics: From the Gold Rush to the Great Depression.* University of Nebraska Press 2011

Conkling, Winifred. *Votes for Women: American Suffragists and the Battle for the Ballot.* Algonquin 2018

Cott, Nancy F. *The Grounding of Modern Feminism.* Yale University Press 1987

Crocco, Margaret Smith, Petra Munro, Kathleen Weiler. *Pedagogies of Resistance: Women Educator Activists, 1880-1960.* Teachers College Press, Columbia University 1999

Davis, Reda. *California Women: A Guide to Their Politics 1885-1911.* California Scene 1968

Enss, Chris. *No Place for a Woman: The Struggle for Suffrage in the Wild West.* TwoDot 2020

Flexner, Eleanor and Ellen Fitzpatrick. *A Century of Struggle.* Belnap Press 1996

Glisson, James and Jennifer Watts. *Nineteen Nineteen.* The Huntington Library 2019

Gullet, Gayle Ann. *Becoming Citizens: The Emergence and Development of the California Woman's Movement 1880-1911.* University of Illinois Press 2000

Haesly, Richard, ed. *Women's Suffrage.* Greenhaven Press 2003

Harper, Ida Husted and Matilda Joslyn Gage. *The History of Women Suffrage.* Andesite Press 2017

Harris, Gloria G. and Hannah S. Cohen. *Women Trailblazers of California: Pioneers to the Present.* The History Press 2012

Hicks, Peter. *Documenting History series. Documenting Women's Suffrage.* Rosen Central 2010

Houde, Mary Jean. *Reaching Out: A Story of the General Federation of Women's Clubs.* The Mobium Press 1989

Jones, Mary Harris. Edited by Mary Field Parton. *The Autobiography of Mother Jones.* Charles H. Kerr Publishing Company 1996

Keller, Kristin Thoennes. *Let Freedom Ring series. The Women Suffrage Movement, 1848-1920.* Bridgestone Books 2003

League of Women Voters of California. *A Sense of Obligation: the Story of the League of Women Voters of California.* 1970

Lunardini, Christine. *Lives of American Women series. Alice Paul: Equality for Women.* Westview Press 2013

Martin, Theodora Penny. *The Sound of Our Own Voices: Women's Study Clubs 1860-1910.* Beacon Press 1987

Mead, Rebecca J. *How the Vote Was Won: Woman Suffrage in the Western United States, 1868-1914.* N. Y. U. Press 2006

O'Gan, Patti. *Traveling for Suffrage: Two Women, a Cat, a Car and a Mission.* National Museum of American History (online article in 4 parts)

Pankhurst, Sylvia. *The Suffragette: The History of the Women's Militant Suffrage Movement.* Dover Publications 1911, 2015

Ryan, Pam Munoz. *Riding Freedom.* Scholastic 1998

Sewell, Jessica Ellen. *Women and the Everyday City: Public Space in San Francisco 1890-1915.* University of Minnesota Press 2011

Seymour, Miranda. *A Ring of Conspirators: Henry James and his Literary Circle 1895-1915.* Houghton Mifflin 1989

Simpson, Lee M. A. *Selling the City: Gender, Class, and the California Growth Machine, 1880-1940.* Stanford University Press 2004

Smith, Sherry. *Bohemians West: Free Love: Family, and Radicals in Twentieth Century America.* Heyday 2020

Southhard, Belinda A. Stillion. *Militant Citizenship: Rhetorical Strategies of the National Woman's Party, 1913-1920.* Texas A & M University Press 2011

Stevens, Doris. Edited by Carol O'Hare. *Jailed for Freedom: American Women Win the Vote.* NewSage Press 1995. [The "Introduction" by Edith Mare, Curator of Political History, Smithsonian Institution, is an excellent capsule history of the movement.]

United States Constitution

Ware, Susan. *American Women's Suffrage: Voices From the Long Struggle for the Vote 1776-1965.* The Library of America 2020

Wells, Mildred White. *Unity in Diversity: The History of the General Federation of Women's Clubs.* General Federation of Women's Club 1953

Wiggin, Kate Douglas. *My Garden of Memory: An Autobiography.* Houghton Mifflin 1923

THE HUNTINGTON LIBRARY BIBLIOGRAPHY

Anthony, Susan B. *Anthony Family collection 1844-1945.*

Apostol, Jane. "Why Women Should Not Have the Vote: Anti-Suffrage Views in the Southland in 1911" *Southern California Quarterly,* v. LXX, #1, Spring 1988.

Berkeley Political Equality Society. *Constitution and By-laws.* 1902

Blackwell, Marilyn S. *Frontier Feminist: Clarina Howard Nichols and the Politics of Motherhood.* University Press of Kansas 2010

Bock, Annie. *Astounded by evils, turns on suffrage: Miss Annie Bock says vote is working havoc among women who have it.* 1918

Burdette, Clara Bradley. *Papers 1843-1954*

— *Letters to Roy B. Wheeler 1880-1923*

California. Adjutant General's Office. *List of Electors, resident of California, in the Military Service of the United States.* 1865

California Citizens. *Petition for Woman's Suffrage: In Senate, March 2, 1870.* D. W. Gelwicks, State Printer 1870

California Community Property Law. Security Trust & Savings Bank, Los Angeles. Trust Department. 1927

California Federation of Business and Professional Women's Clubs. *The California Woman.* San Francisco n.d.

California Federation of Women's Clubs. *California Clubwoman.* 1948

California Federation of Women's Clubs. *California the Land of Dreams: A Pageant Presented at the Twentieth Annual Convention, 1921*

California Federation of Women's *Clubs. California Federation News.* n. d.

California Federation of Women's Clubs. *The First Convention of the California Federation of Women's Clubs February 4-7, 1902.*

California Federation of Women's Clubs. Los Angeles District. *Foreign Arts and Crafts Exhibit Under the Auspices of The Americanization Department of the Los Angeles District.* 1921

California Federation of Women's Clubs. [Collection of leaflets and pamphlets 1917-1937]

California Federation of Women's Clubs. *Historic Facts and Fancies: History and Landmarks Section of California Federation of Women's Clubs.* 1907

— *Reports*…1917. Berkeley, Calif.

— Committee of Political Science. *A Survey of the Results of Woman Suffrage in California.* 1917

California. Legislature. Assembly. Committee on Petition for Woman's Suffrage, *Recommending an Amendment to the State Constitution.* 1870

California. Legislature. Assembly. Committee on the memorial of the California Woman Suffrage Association. *Report of the Assembly Committee to which was referred the memorial of the California Woman Suffrage Association.* 1876

California. Legislature. Assembly. Special Committee in Relation to Granting Women Political Equality. *Report.* T. A. Spring, State Printer 1872

California. Legislature. Joint Committee on the Memorial of the California Woman's Suffrage Association. *Report.* 1874

California. Supreme Court. *The Soldier's Vote. The Leading and Dissenting Opinions of the Supreme Court.* 1863

California Woman's Suffrage Association. *Constitution and By-Laws.* 1902

— *Report of the Assembly Committee, to which was referred the memorial of the California Woman Suffrage Association.* 1876

Carpenter, Ed., comp. *Los Angeles, 200 Years.* Henry E. Huntington Library 1981

Chandler, Mr. Edward M. *Remarks*. Pennsylvania Limited Suffrage League 1912

The Citizen's handbook containing the registry act, the constitutional provisions defining the right of suffrage, and the laws regulation elections. 1866

Club Woman. Los Angeles n.d.

Club Women of California State Register and Directors 1906-10. The Independent Press

Coolidge, Mary Roberts. *What the Women of California Have Done With the Ballot.* California Civic League 1916

College Equal Suffrage League of Northern California. *Winning Equal Suffrage in California,* National College Equal Suffrage League 1913

Cott, Nancy R. *The Grounding of Modern Feminism.* Yale University Press 1989

Crocker, H. S. & Co. *Crocker's Guide for Election Officers.* 1890

Davis, Reda. *The Life of Marietta Stow, Cooperator.* Pt. Pinos Editions 1980

Diary of a Trip to California 1911

DuBois, Ellen and Karen Kearns. *Votes for Women: A 75th Anniversary Album.* Huntington Library 1995

DuBois, Ellen. *Feminism and Suffrage: The Emergence of an Independent Women's Movement in America.* Cornell University Press 1999

Edwards. Rebecca. *Angels in the Machinery: Gender in American Party Politics from the Civil War to the Progressive Era.* Oxford University Press 1997

Elinson, Elaine and Stan Yogi. *Wherever There's a Fight: How Runaway Slaves, Suffragists, Immigrants, Strikers, and Poets Shaped Civil Liberties in California.* Heyday Books 2009

Englander, Susan. *Class Coalition and Class Conflict in the California Woman Suffrage Movements 1907-1912.* Mellen Research University Press 1992

Field, Sara Bart. *Poet and Suffragist. Interview by Amelia R. Fry.* Berkeley, CA, Regional Oral History Office, Bancroft Library, University of California, Berkeley 1979

Foltz, Clara S. *Brief on the Constitutionality of Senate Bill No. 266: Being an Act Entitled "An act to enable women to vote at elections for school officers, and in matters pertaining solely to the schools, and to qualify them to hold educational offices," presented by request to the Senate Committee on Elections of the 25th session of the California Legislature.* Lewis & Johnston, printers 1883

Friday Morning Club Los Angeles. *Records* 1770-2012

Gibson, Mary. *A Record of Twenty-Five Years of California Federation of Women's Clubs 1900-1925.* California Federation of Women's Clubs 1927.

Gilman, Charlotte Perkins. *Women and Economics: A Study of the Economic Relations Between Men and Women as a Factor in Social Evolution.* Small, Maynard & Co 1898

Glisson, James and Jennifer A. Watts. *Nineteen Nineteen.* The Huntington Library, Art Collections and Botanical Gardens 2019

Harbert, Elizabeth Boynton. *Papers* 1863-1925

Harris, Gloria G. and Hannah Cohen. *Women Trailblazers of California: Pioneers to the Present.* History Press 2012

Higby, William. *Remarks of Hon. William Higby, of California, in the House of Representatives,* 1860

Hill, Daniel Elis. *As Seen in Vogue.* Texas Tech University Press 2004.

Hutton, Frankie, ed. *Outsiders in 19th-Century Press History: Multicultural Perspectives.* Bowling Green State University Popular Press 1995

International Woman Suffrage Alliance Congress. *Third Congress Program, Copenhagen, Denmark, 1906*

International Woman Suffrage Alliance Congress. *Seventh Congress Program, Budapest, June 15-29, 1913*

International Woman Suffrage Alliance. *Tenth Congress Program. Paris, May 30-June 6, 1926. Headquarters of the Alliance, London, 1926*

International Woman Suffrage Conference. First International Woman Suffrage Conference, and the 34th Annual Convention of the National American Woman Suffrage Association held in the First Presbyterian Church, Washington, D. C. Feb. 12-18, 1902

Janin Family Papers 1735-1932

McNeil, Rusty and Keith, compliers and editors. *California Songbook.* WEM Records 2001

Marquis, Neeta. *Papers 1862-1957*

Marilley, Suzanne M. *Woman Suffrage and its Origins of a Liberal Feminism in the United States 1820-1920.* Harvard University Press 1996

Massachusetts Association Opposed to the Further Extension of Suffrage to Women. *Remonstrance Against Woman Suffrage.* July 1912

Memories of the Days of Old, Days of Gold, Days of 49. The Banner Print 1923

Miller, Dorothy Grace. *Within the Bounds of Propriety: Clara Burdette and the Woman's Movement.* 1984

Laws of California *Relating to Women and Children/ Offered to the State of California by Mrs. Willo.* Baumgardt Pub. Co. 1911

National American Woman. Warren, Ohio Headquarters. *Series of Leaflets.* 1900-1910

Noel, Frances Nacke and Job Harriman. *Papers, 1889-1986.*

Nunis, Jr., Doyce B., ed. *Women in the Life of Southern California.* Historical Society of Southern California 1996

Park, Alice. *Papers 1798-1953*

Parkman, Francis. *Some of the reasons against woman suffrage: printed at the request of an association of women.* Santa Susana Press, California State University 1977

Paul, Alice. *Conversations with Alice Paul: woman suffrage and the Equal Rights Amendment / an interview conducted by Amelia R. Fry.* Regional Oral History Office, University of California Berkeley 1976

Rankin, Jeannette. *Activist for World Peace, women's rights and democratic government. Interview.* Bancroft Library, University of California Berkeley 1974

Riley, Glenda and Richard W. Etulain, eds. *By Grit & Grace: Eleven Women Who Shaped the American West.* Fulcrum Publishing 1997

Sanford, John B. *Extracts from a speech against women suffrage in the California State Senate.* 1912

Schaffer, Ronald. *Problem of Consciousness in the Woman Suffrage Movement: a California Perspective, 1932*

Scharff, Virginia. *Twenty Thousand Roads: Women, Movement and the West.* University of California Press 2003

Seagraves, Anne. *High-Spirited Women of the West.* Wesanne Publications 1992

Severance, Caroline Maria Seymour. *Caroline Severance Letter to Mrs. J. E. Smith.* May 1906

— *Extra Session of California Legislature v.2:2.* National American Women Suffrage Association 1896

— *Papers 1830-1980*

Sewell, Jessica Ellen. *Women and the Everyday City: Public Space in San Francisco, 1890-1915.* University of Minnesota Press 2011

Shirpser, Clara. *Behind the Scenes in Politics: The Memoirs of Clara Shirpser.* American Lives Endowment 1981

Silver, Mae. *The Sixth Star.* Ord Street Press 2000

Simons, Seward A., Mrs. *A Survey of the Results of Women Suffrage in California.* California Federation of Women's Clubs 1917

Solomons, Selina. *The Girl from Colorado: or, The Conversation of Aunty Suffridge: a Playlet with a Purpose.* Votes-for-Women Pub. Co. 1911 [Interesting one-hour play]

— *How We Won the Vote in California: A True Story of the Campaign of 1911.* The New Woman Pub. Co. 1912

Spencer, Dorcas James. *A History of the Woman's Christian Temperance Union of Northern and Central California.* West Coast Printing Co. 1913

Stanley, Sara Marie. *Caroline M. Severance: Feminist and Reformer 1820-1914.* 1978

Stetson, Charlotte Perkins [Gilman]. *Women and Economics: A Study of the Economic Relations Between Men and Women as a Factor in Social Evolution.* Small, Maynard & Co. 1898

Stow, Mrs. J. W. *Probate Chaff, or, Beautiful Probate; or, Three Years Probating in San Francisco. A Modern Drama.* Stow 1879

— *Probate Confiscation: And The Unjust Laws Which Govern Women.* Bacon & Company Printers 1876

Suffrage Songs. 1891-1915

Susan B. Anthony Memorial Committee of California, comp. and ed. *Alice Park of California: Worker for Woman Suffrage and for Children's Rights.* 1948

— *Susan B. Anthony Memorial Collections, 1798-1954.* [Includes: Photographs, prints, and ephemera boxes 1-3; California Clippings [scrapbooks] v. 1-6; Clippings [scrapbooks]

A Survey of the Results of Woman Suffrage in California.

Todd, Emma G. *Pinxit, or Portraits of Modern Politics.* 1894

Vernon, Mabel. *Speaker for Suffrage and Petitioner for Peace/ Mabel Vernon: an interview conducted by Amelia R. Fry.* Regional Oral History Office, Bancroft Library, University of California, Berkeley 1976

Vose Stearns McCormick Family Papers 1834-1953

Wallis, Eileen V. *Earning Power: Women and Work in Los Angeles, 1889-1930.* University of Nevada Press 2010

Ware, Susan, editor. *American Women's Suffrage: Voices from the Long Struggle for the Vote 1776-1965.* The Library of America 2020

Watkins, Louise Ward. *Papers, 1871-1974*

Weinberg, Arthur, ed. *Passport to Utopia: Great Panaceas in American History.* Quadrangle / the New York Times Book Co. 1978

Wiggin, Kate Douglas. *The Girl and the Kingdom: Learning to Teach. Notes on the Development of the Kindergarten in California.* Printed by the Local Convention Committee for Presentation to the Members of the International Kindergarten Union in Convention at Los Angeles, California July 8-11, 1925.

Winter, Una Richardson. *Alice Park of California: Worker for Woman Suffrage and for Children's Rights.* 1942

— *Papers 1895-1954*

— *Photograph Collection 1860-1930*

The Woman's Appeal to the Voters of California: Do Not Vote for the Woman Suffrage Amendment! 1911

Wood, Charles Erskine Scott. *Papers* 1829-1980

Wood, Mary I. *The History of the General Federation of Women's Clubs.* New York: History Dept., General Federation of Women's Clubs, 1912

The Yellow Ribbon. [newspaper] published by Katherine Reed Balentine. n. d.

www.ingramcontent.com/pod-product-compliance
Lightning Source LLC
LaVergne TN
LVHW022313200926
848481LV00004B/1319
9798349404290